SPOT

WEATHER

FORECAST

10 9 8 7 6 5 4 3 2 1

Alice James Books are published by Alice James Poetry Cooperative, Inc., an affiliate of the
University of Maine at Farmington.

Alice James Books
114 Prescott Street
Farmington, ME 04938
www.alicejamesbooks.org

Library of Congress Cataloging-in-Publication Data

Names: Goodan, Kevin, 1969- author.
Title: Spot weather forecast / Kevin Goodan.
Description: Farmington, ME : Alice James Books, [2021]
Identifiers: LCCN 2021009343 (print) | LCCN 2021009344 (ebook) | ISBN
    9781948579223 (trade paperback) | ISBN 9781948579469 (epub)
Subjects: LCSH: Fire fighters--Poetry. | LCGFT: Poetry.
Classification: LCC PS3607.O563 S66 2021 (print) | LCC PS3607.O563
    (ebook) | DDC 811/.6--dc23
LC record available at https://lccn.loc.gov/2021009343
LC ebook record available at https://lccn.loc.gov/2021009344

Alice James Books gratefully acknowledges support from individual donors, private foundations, the
University of Maine at Farmington, the National Endowment for the Arts, the Amazon Literary Partnership,
and the Maine Arts Commission, an independent state agency supported by the
National Endowment for the Arts.

Cover art: "Night Fire" by Stephen Quiller, www.quillergallery.com

SPOT WEATHER FORECAST:

A FIRE LITURGY

KEVIN GOODAN

Alice James Books
Farmington, Maine
www.alicejamesbooks.org

CONTENTS

For RJ Nomee

But my soul is a fire that suffers if it does not blaze.

—Stendhal

Fire Storm. Fire behavior is extremely violent. Diameters have been observed to be from 1,000 to 10,000 feet and winds estimated in excess of 110 MPH. This is a rare phenomenon and hopefully one that is so unlikely in the forest environment that it can be disregarded.

David W. Goens, "Fire Whirls,"
National Weather Service, 1978

Because the first condition of the universe is fire
Because fire is the emergence and culmination of a cycle
Because fire is a product of rise over run
Because fire itself is narrative
Because the correlation of breathing in the proximity of flame
    is part of the story
Because we purse our lips to intensity
Because of the angle of the body to ash
Because the Pulaski is the vehicle of the power
Because the power is gained in its arc
Because shins are rock-bruised and bloody
Because the legs do not flinch anymore at the tool's deflection
Because adrenaline is a feast for the body, brain euphoric
Because fear is the instinct
Because the crown fire is above you
Because fire can double back on an anchor point
Because the chinking of tools in rocks grows syncopated and
    scattered
Because our very breath is fuel to the fire
(Little bird, little bird, do not spirit away)
Because our labor is an orchestration
Because our weather girl is six foot three with a full beard
and answers to Toad
Because Toad takes weather every half hour, then fifteen
    minutes, then is constantly
        Swinging the gauge: good Toad, bad Toad, fuck
Because the burnout operation from the river to the ridge is
    our symphony
(At once, two birds of flame rise outside the line)
Because the underside of crown fire is fire

Because we smack-talk the flame front to resist its trancing convections
Because it is there, always there: my urge to enter the fire.

When the fire says remember,
I say: First manifestation,
Crop fire. In such smoke
I lost my way on the road.
Calling: Grandpa, Grandpa
Save me now. The Fear
And hot bitter air made
My three-year-old body skitter
Then balk. Flames whorled,
Skirted around me, said:
We have much to teach you,
Little brother. Then
An ember seared me
high up, between the shoulder blades.
A mark. I carry it still.

Most believe flames are greedy, indiscriminate,
Consume what lies in their path. Flames choose
What feeds them: this drainage, not that; this house,
But not others around it; this body crowned in fire
While the rest are taken bit by bit. At night we dream
The ignition, all the homonyms of action, the wrinkled air
Holding, for a moment, what used to be: gated wyes,
A King radio melting between coordinates to safety,
A buckle, scrap, of belt, a few threads of canvas
Where the pack skidded along, strip of boot, a glove.
The unconsumed, and the unconceived, are we not
Inheritors of ash, the colors of now, the land
In its rending? That which is brittle, has ruptured,
Cracked, germinated, taken root in us, have these not
Blurred the haunting? Horsemen, horsemen, I hear you near,
The sound—blades dig through rock, this body, the others.

Whose throat does not house
A conflagration? Whose lungs
Do not feel the mortal twinge
Shiver a breath from them?
I look down into the valley
Of my life, cupping an ear
To hear the sudden chorus
Of trees ignite, the refrain
To overtake the draw—
For such roaring is a proverb
A distraction of light—
Singe me, I whisper
As I let that fire catch me now
And purge me into songlets of ash.

We dream coniferous—
Thick ropes of smoke
That braid into a weather
Of reignited ash.
We use our lips
As guides to the small air
Beyond our seeing—
Who was it said
Throw your tools
Then laughed into the handheld?
Who was it that stumbled,
Puked, and muttered, Leave me,
Leave me? Who turned
And calmly walked through
The flame? Whose face
Is it now that wakes me
Smoke-blind, fear-slobbered,
Swatting the embers
That burn into the neck,
The backs of knees, cuffs,
And every glove—
Who are you running toward me
Beneath the canopy of ghost-trees?

Everything we did had to do with lines.
We slept in lines, we dreamed in lines,
We fixed ourselves to lines on the map.
We flung our line gear on, lined out
On the slope to dig handline, hotline,
Jumperline, scratchline the best we could.
We kept our lines of communication open.
We called in longlines, laid down blackline,
Anchored our lines to natural breaks,
Sweat running down our bodies in lines.
At night, inside our lines, we hunkered
Around the smoldering stumps, whispering
The day amongst ourselves, gear laid out
In lines.

A tree's second dream
Is fire—
O wreck of air
The sacred collision
A day divines—
If I step
Will God's weight
Crush me?
Pin my wings
Name me star—
I am the burning guide
That covets every flame.

Where are you now
Great churning storms
We rebuffed with our bodies
And a few handmade tools?
And when we taunted you
With gestures, how were we
To know we were the ones
Still being forged
In the breath of stars?

We step from the ash
And ghosts greet us
With rough hands
From across the line,
Wanting their names
To be spoken in the
Still and darkening air.
And when we say,
Fisher, Stamm, Mackey,
Touchette, they crack
Their ghost-smiles
And guide us back toward
The pale and waiting flames.

The steep slope ripples
In radiant heat, sudden
Ignitions of buckbrush
Here, there, we position,
We prepare the line   .
Underslung, overburden
Flung, radios crackle
At our chests, we spray
Water to the base of flame,
We turn our heads when
Heat is painful, all warning
Before rupture comes, we
Exhale, spit tobacco, guffaw,
Wince, pray, we move to
The black, someone throws
A drip torch, we read
The loopy script of its falling,
Take in what it conveys,
What prophecy, what
Drivel, we say, Fate is no
Here, just the sweated, the bleeding.

Sting of that fire elemental
Of the many-tongued flame-to-be
And of that blaze set always
Between you and me: the blue-rooted
Flame, the mother-of-pearl-flicker,
The radiant-glazed, gradient-whorled,
The updraft-wafted, drought-kilned,
The beetle-killed-kindled, smoke-
Tendrilled, slope-addled, stop-haunted,
Spoor-mottled, budworm-brittled,
Fungus-fluttered, bole-blasted,
Lightning-licked, root-rot-ringed,
Fire, fire, fir, the dry, dry air alone—
The ember-suckled, cold-cell-nurtured,
The gust-granted, the buckbrush-muffled,
The beargrass-bejeweled, the kinnikinnik-
Strewn, the ladder-fueled, the tenuous-
Rooted, cambial-scorched, the drip-torched,
Saw-kerfed, shovel-scraped, all the singe-
Worthy duff, and you (ah!) my lord, STING.

"At 1230 June 25th, a dry lightning storm started a fire under the Mogollon Rim on the Payson Ranger District, Tonto NF Arizona. The fire was on a steep SW facing slope at 6,400 ft. elevation. At 1330, the fire was estimated from the air at 5 acres, 50 acres one hour later, and over 100 acres by 1615 with a spot fire one mile east of the main fire. By 1800 a Type II IMT had arrived and a Type I IMT and 18 crews had been ordered. Brisk down canyon winds pushed the fire, and it was 1,900 acres by 0500 on June 26th and was threatening the forest subdivision of Bonita Creek Estates. A convection column, aided by combustion, began forming over the fire by 1000. The column continued to grow and became a fully mature thunderstorm by 1400. Radio and frequency issues caused a breakdown in communication between the crews and the overhead team. The teams transition mid-shift resulted in confusion between the crews and supervision. The thunderstorm also began to decay creating strong downbursts channeled by the topography. This caused dramatic down- and cross-slope fire spread on nearly all sides of the fire. Members of the Perryville Fire Crew would not be able to escape from the fast and erratic fire spread. Five were injured. Six died on the fireline."

—Incident Summary, The Dude Fire, June 26, 1990

Downtown Marshall Brown loopy
From lack of sleep, fumbling
To load the Very pistol,
Our dumpster-diving crew foreman,
Our mashed-faced Hephaestus
Stumbling splayfooted, raw-kneed
Through deadfall, rubbing
His malformed cheek
With the back of his sweat-sopped glove,
Hunching to aim, shouting:
Yeah baby, fuckin' A yeah, burn it,
Burn it the fuck all.

We scan for patterans of ignition,
Slips of smoke tainting the far dark trees,
Which is the message: Spot fire, hold-
Over, or a man insane with wind—
We read the map to know what names
Are fixed to topography: Bitch Creek,
Deadman Gulch, Spook Peak—
We mark latitude, spitball longitude,
Recalibrate our eyes to the grids,
Our subtle visions, the syntax
Of emergent flame.

When the holding-wood pops
And the snag sets back
Twisting the peewee wedge
Out of the back-cut, there is
That singular moment
Looking up the narrowing length
Of barkless trunk that the light
Shivers at the crown
And the body pauses
And the saw pauses
Before torquing from your hands
And even though the snag
Is spinning toward you
You watch the light coming down—
Bright ash, bright ash, flesh.

Sun purpled at its apex.
Strange wind twisting trees
Before they ignite, convection
Killing the buckbrush, white berries
Bursting into char. This is now,
The journey in which nothing
Is augury and what is called Fate
Resides in the aleatoric of flame.
Here is the language of incineration.
How far can a body run
When it's encased in fire?
How do we convey the transference
Into ash? To trap, to keep what is
Known to us? What do we do
When all the thousand-hour fuels
Have ignited? When crews
Were finally able to recover
The bodies, they found broken
The fingers in each gloved hand.

The first language is of fire.
The scorching is fleeting
But scars do not fade
From the branding as we are
Drawn upward to the light.

I am feral, brunt-of-storm
Red Flag Warning
Suck and sear of the crowning
Ember-flinging
Dry slope torching—
Eye to the ridgeline
For I bring no route to safety
And the scorching at mine flanks
Shall be uncontainable
And the flames from mine head
Shall be thy roiling baptism.

"They stated that all of a sudden the entire area was on fire and they barely had time to get around and under the dozer. In their haste they left their shelters on the dozer track.

Neither individual could remember how long they had stayed under the dozer, but from best recollection, it seemed about 30 minutes. During that time, they experienced very harsh fire behavior, strong and gusty winds, flying embers, dust and a period where breathing became very difficult from what seemed like a reduction of oxygen.

In the interview, they claimed because things got so hectic, they did not have enough time to deploy fire shelters. The best the two individuals could do was to throw dirt on each other to keep the embers from burning them. Featherly did have a fire shirt and pants, and adequate footwear and gloves. Kramer had a fire shirt, but had Levi jeans and had lost his gloves in the excitement. The crew lacked goggles, and did not deploy shelters."

—Virginia Lake Fire Entrapment, August 13, 2001
Incident Overview

Some Hi-toned fire gods
Who believe
In outflow
The giver of flames,
Who proceeds from the falter
The tonnage of air
Plosive to the tongue.
Glory be to the ladder fuels,
The crown fire flaring
(King me, O most high)
In mysteries of topography,
The profession of updraft—
Fireheart, Breathburn,
Gods exhalted
And terrified
In the sanctity of risk
The taste of it
Hallelujah—
In the progressions
Of flame,
In digging
Fourteen miles
Of hotline
In eleven days.

"My pack was flailing behind me, really slowing me down. So I dropped it, grabbed the shelter out of the side pocket and had it under my arm, with my radio in one hand and my hard hat and GPS in the other." [Roy had grabbed his hardhat and GPS along with his radio when he first left the truck. In the rush, he never had the time to put the hard hat on.]

"It occurred to me they weren't doing me any good either, so I dropped them (hard hat and GPS). It also occurred to me that my shelter wasn't doing any good in the plastic case. It'd be pretty stupid if they found me like that, shelter still in the case under my arm."

—Horse Park Fire Entrapment, May 27, 2018, Logan IHC
Superintendent Roy

Jet boats ferry us up the Salmon River as far as they can and we clamber off, portion out gear to hike the fourteen miles to the ignition site of a rolling twenty-thousand-acre fire. We arrive sweating in the dark and sleep where we can in the dirt by the river. When we wake, we see poison ivy. Sixty men, three shot crews look at each other, wondering what will come of it, and when. By the second day digging hotline, our arms begin to boil and blister and the poison ivy is growing everywhere, on the ground, around trees, in the smoke. Our Nomex is saturated with the oils. Sweat smears the oils around. Blisters on the face, blisters in the nose. Someone goes blind in the smoke, and we breathe it in. Lips blister, tongues blister, some can't swallow from blisters in the throat. On the fourth day, we are digging line and sloughing our skin. Everyone tries their hardest not to take a dump because assholes are blistered, the weepy pouches breaking and breaking. The foremen call in a supply manifest and on that list is Clorox. When it arrives, we start pouring bleach over the hanging skin of our arms. One guy is so crazed from the itch he tries to gargle bleach before someone does the Heimlich on him mid-scream. And still, we hike and dig from before first light until after dark.

"At 1520, H-166 said it was coming to get the rappellers at H-2 but couldn't land because of the smoke. Lead plane 41 heard the rappellers on H-2 respond to H-166 in a calm voice that the winds were 20 to 25 knots and that they were leaving H-2. At 1524, the rappellers called and asked, "Could I get a helicopter up right now?" Lead plane 41 observed that when the fire in the Cache Bar drainage reached the ridge, some flame lengths were 50 feet or more with occasional flame lengths up to 100 feet. The fire, described as "a big flash front," burned over and around H-2, killing the rappellers shortly after their last radio transmission. Estimated temperatures at the fatality site were from 1,300 °F to potentially over 2,000 °F. Two fire shelters were found at the site, but neither was deployed."

—Management Evaluation Report, Cramer Fire,
July 22, 2003

We give
Our lungs
To the fire,
Their frothy
Pink and
Trembling
Capacities.
The hinge-work
Of our knees
Also.
What's good
Of our backs
We give,
Disks in
The spine
Flattened,
Springing
To the nerves.
Shoulders
Tendon-bright,
Straining
The sockets.
We give
Bruise, we
Give gash
Whatever
Bleeds, bleeds—
Shinbones
Divoted
From tool-blows,

Armpits raw
From sweat-rimed
Nomex
Grating under
Line gear straps,
Heels
Blister-jelled,
Popping,
Back of neck
Seared, glistered.
Give ankles
Hobbled,
Ligaments
Tattered
Sutured
Tattered.
Skin we give
To ember,
To aramids,
To the long
Memory
Cancer has.
Ears given
To squelch,
Break,
Rotor wash,
A far voice
Calling
Weakly
For water

For god
Who is
Water
Out there
In the
Brittle woods.
Give lips
Heat-crazed
Blubbering
Double-time
Double-time,
Water
Boiling
From eyes,
Lashes
Rancid nubs,
A beard,
Moustache
Smoldering,
Tobacco spit,
Tobacco
Slobber.
Fingers
In gloves
In ash
Swollen,
Putty
To the bone,
Lactic surge
In arms

In calves
As we pause
Swiping back
The grime-slicked hair
Then bending
To our
Ash-dark art
Once more.

The small nits of fire
Are pithy and fast, aren't they?
And we are not afraid
Of their flockings,
The way they alight on piss-fir
And swarm manic, correct?
When little things come to our skin,
Singe our hair, we let them,
Don't we? Never asking what
Is coaxed from our flesh, what is wicked.
What the nits say is hunger.
That is the passion of incineration,
Yes? The scabs they leave,
The scars they own
Are their homes in our bodies,
The alchemy of form into flame.
And we laugh, and don't we taunt,
Raising our fists to the radiants,
To the spirals of fire we are
Trapped by.

We station ourselves along the slope.
We've calculated wind shift,
The fire's own need for air.
When the radios click we uncap
Our flare and strike them,
Breathing in sulfuric puffs
As the neon flames spurt
To the thick brush we light,
Making a fire that marries fire
And halts it. We daub our flares
Here and there, scribe intentions
On the dark where every move
Becomes a function of light,
A cursive that whispers our names
To the overstory as we double-click
Our mics, strapped to our chests
Like crucifixes that guide us
Through the night-burn, back
Into our dreams again.

And the flame
Hovered there
Above hard hats
Sucking air
From our lungs
And each body
Locked in fear
Of what was
Happening
And in that moment
No one lived
Apart from the other
And the voice
We heard was not
Our voice
But a sudden
And fierce blooming—
And our eyes
Bore witness,
Our flesh
Bore witness,
Little burns,
Supple blisters
And our hair
Bore witness
In wreaths
Of smoke

And when darkness came
We hiked again
Upslope, each step
That brightness
Flaring inside us.

In the conditions of the name
Thin breeze of the name
In the heat of the name
Gust of the name
Single-digit humidity of it
In the pine beetle of the name
In the rise over run of the name
In the sear of the name
In the flare of the name
Back-burn of the name
The flanking of the name
The hurt of it, the name
In the anchor point
In the hotline
In the laterals of the name
Drip torch of the name
Blivet of the name
The slurry of it, the name
In the lean, the face-cut of the name
Skip chain of the name
Flat file of it
In spike camp of the name
In the VRTOL of the name
Jolly Green Giant of the name
P2V and TBM of it
In the phlegm of the name
In the bruise of the name
Sweat of the name
The blister of it, your name.

What is in our ears is blood. What we hear
Are trees igniting, firebrands in our beards
As we search for pockets of cool air,
The struggling musculature awash with
The acids of can't-go-on
And carry-me, carry-me.
Bodies before us blur.
Bodies behind us blear in the energy
As we scurry the slope
And when a ligament snaps in the knee
There is nothing to do—
Wince, yell,
Yell and run.

That the flames are echo chambers for the lost.

That whomever is lost shall lie down in their voices
Through the intercession of fire.

That in the body there shall be a twisting, a rending into
light.

Ash in the mouth.
Ash in the saying.

The pyrocumulus
Is a fickle beast,
Smoke and char
Puncturing air,
Drawing up into
Its body all manner
Of heat, until
Head heavy with ice
There is pause
In its appetite.
When the hairs
On your neck go flat
With calm, when
Flames set back
Say what prayer you want:
This is your warning.
Check your Pulaski.
Check radio, check
Canteen. Three hundred
Yards up the draw
To safety, give or take.
You have your lungs,
Have your legs.
Your Shake 'n Bake
Is last resort
And might just
Cook you golden brown.
When the plume
Caves in, wind
Can't get away from itself

Fast enough, as if
Trapdoors in the tiers
Of heaven drop
And the outflow
That blasts you down
Ain't nobody's angel,
Is pure detonation,
A concussive wave
Of scorch uprooting trees,
Flaying unburned fuels
to char, obliterating
The stag, who in his fear
Turns, and leaps into flame.
And here you are
Back at the beginning
Of the universe, mumbling
Your prayer in your
Upslope hobble,
Believing some hand
Will save you. Here,
You are on your own.

Morning finds us
A slight easterly breeze
Twirling up ash
From the far ridge
Laid bare last night
In a back-burn.
Sweat beads up,
Grit on forearms,
Tools, fresh-filed, flash
The purpled sun.
Upslope we tread
The trough of hotline—
Buckbrush roots,
Pulaskied back to the
Overburden, glisten.
Wounds on our shins
Darken. We hike on
Past the char of deer
Beginning to reek—
Turkey buzzards swoop
Then veer. Beargrass
Twists its smolder,
The punky duff. Above
The thermal belt
We pause. Particulate
Layers lift from the draw
And the water we drink
Lifts from our pores,
A salty halo catching
The light. We tune

Radios to the spot
Weather forecast,
The complex parameters
Of the County Line Fire.
We hike on, ears
Twitching for a whistle
That is a snag coming down
After Szabo took one
Yesterday, smashing
His shoulder to mush.

O illuminated realms / plumes / voices
Squelching / hear me / we are
Somewhere.

After dry MRE sausage patties, we line out
To hike from Spike Camp Bravo into
The drainage to construct indirect line for
A burnout, when Boomer halts, twirls, gibbers,
Throws off his saw, and with his bowie knife
Begins stabbing the fabric at his sides.
He reaches into the front of his Nomex
And jerks out the tatters of his leopard-print
Bikini underwear. He shakes his legs, smiles,
And whistling "We're off to See the Wizard,"
Hikes on.

We scout for natural breaks
In the understory and build
Line toward them:
Scree slope, bare ridge,
Logging unit, previous
Signatures of scarification
Against which we gauge
Rates of spread, firebrands
And their calling:
Every corner of the Fire
Triangle ignited.
We work as a unity,
Twenty segments of a body
Thriving on dirt, terrain,
Embers and ashes
And this implosion
Where Fuck is the mantra,
The blue calm
At the base of flames.

At Morning Briefing, the Incident Commander
Pulls our crew aside for secret duty. So, we bus
Down to the river, grid out, searching for
The boy missing from a campground.
We start the grid reluctant, calling the boy's name,
Voices strange with the sound of it. Twenty of us
With the same dry taste in our mouths. We halt
While one examines a shrub. We halt while one
Examines a hollowed snag. We halt for a plastic
Bag in sagebrush. Halt for the way frost is melting.
For deer ribs beneath a pine. None of us wants
To find the boy, to see whatever pale, small thing
Has hung up in the log jam, down there,
At the bend in the river.

Who will contest
The ownership
Of fire? Trees
Murmur to each
Other: Torque
The fire. We
Are burning.

At H-4, Division Delta,
we huddle in a reeky air of soot, char,
Flesh unwashed and waxy
In Nomex and line gear
As we scan the mosaic
Of the dwindling fire:
False draw scathed,
Wet draw seared,
Islands of green
Below the thermal belt.
Some open the last MREs,
Hoard tiny Tabasco bottles.
Some sharpen tools,
Repack gear, calculate
The manifest, the weight
Of each sling load. Some
Tune to chatter on the handheld,
Squelch out codes:
Helibase, Helitack, Strike Team,
Cat 2 Crews, Con Crews,
Digger Squad, Bucket Drops,
Leadplane, Dozer Boss—
So many names in the smoke
As the inversion sloughs
Toward us, we who torched
this Eden, and will again.

What we render is what we become
No matter how we read the air
For ghost-tongues, the bitter
Blinding, binding words
Fueling this blue world
And we plead the horizon
Every division of light
Every black snag that is
The memory of what has come
And we look for what is leaning,
What's fallen within the forests
Of ourselves, the far deepening
Glimpse of what some say is
The fingerprint of God
Now the fires have gone.

I stand at the fire
Of my own making
Calculating
Flame length
Rate of spread—
Gather tinder
More fine fuels
So the heat
Will punch through
This inversion,
Enter the upper airs.
I wander wobbly
Scrounging
Hundred-hour fuels
To sustain the burning
Til the fire calls me in.

Molecules of smoke
That declare your flame—
Vision! Vision! Amen.

ACKNOWLEDGMENTS

The author would like to thank the following journals for publishing poems from this book, sometimes in earlier manifestations:

Poetry Daily
Poetry Northwest
Terrain.org
San Pedro River Review

I would also like to express gratitude to the following people for providing a sustaining and critical discourse about this work: Kimberly Burwick, Rebecca Gayle Howell, and Adam Ottavi.

Gratitude also to the Lolo Interagency Hotshot Crew for the foundational experiences of this work.

RECENT TITLES FROM ALICE JAMES BOOKS

How to Not Be Afraid of Everything, Jane Wong
Brocken Spectre, Jacques J. Rancourt
No Ruined Stone, Shara McCallum
The Vault, Andrés Cerpa
White Campion, Donald Revell
Last Days, Tamiko Beyer
If This Is the Age We End Discovery, Rosebud Ben-Oni
Pretty Tripwire, Alessandra Lynch
Inheritance, Taylor Johnson
The Voice of Sheila Chandra, Kazim Ali
Arrow, Sumita Chakraborty
Country, Living, Ira Sadoff
Hot with the Bad Things, Lucia LoTempio
Witch, Philip Matthews
Neck of the Woods, Amy Woolard
Little Envelope of Earth Conditions, Cori A. Winrock
Aviva-No, Shimon Adaf, Translated by Yael Segalovitz
Half/Life: New & Selected Poems, Jeffrey Thomson
Odes to Lithium, Shira Erlichman
Here All Night, Jill McDonough
To the Wren: Collected & New Poems, Jane Mead
Angel Bones, Ilyse Kusnetz
Monsters I Have Been, Kenji C. Liu
Soft Science, Franny Choi
Bicycle in a Ransacked City: An Elegy, Andrés Cerpa
Anaphora, Kevin Goodan
Ghost, like a Place, Iain Haley Pollock
Isako Isako, Mia Ayumi Malhotra
Of Marriage, Nicole Cooley
The English Boat, Donald Revell
We, the Almighty Fires, Anna Rose Welch
DiVida, Monica A. Hand
pray me stay eager, Ellen Doré Watson

Alice James Books is committed to publishing books that matter. The press was founded in 1973 in Boston, Massachusetts as a cooperative, wherein authors performed the day-to-day undertakings of the press. This element remains present today, as authors who publish with the press are invited to collaborate closely in the publication process of their work. AJB remains committed to its founders' original feminist mission, while expanding upon the scope to include all voices and poets who might otherwise go unheard. In keeping with its efforts to build equity and increase inclusivity in publishing and the literary arts, AJB seeks out poets whose writing possesses the range, depth, and ability to cultivate empathy in our world and to dynamically push against silence. The press was named for Alice James, sister to William and Henry, whose extraordinary gift for writing went unrecognized during her lifetime.

Designed by
PAMELA A. CONSOLAZIO

Spark
design

PRINTED BY MCNAUGHTON & GUNN